To my precious cousin Holly:
You remind me daily that I am treasured!

You are...

You are
helpful.

You are friendly.

You are
a good listener.

You are
lovely.

You are
strong.

You are
self-less.

You are
enough.

You are special.

Thank You!

You are
appreciated.

You are
a superhero.

You are
the
executive
of your
life.

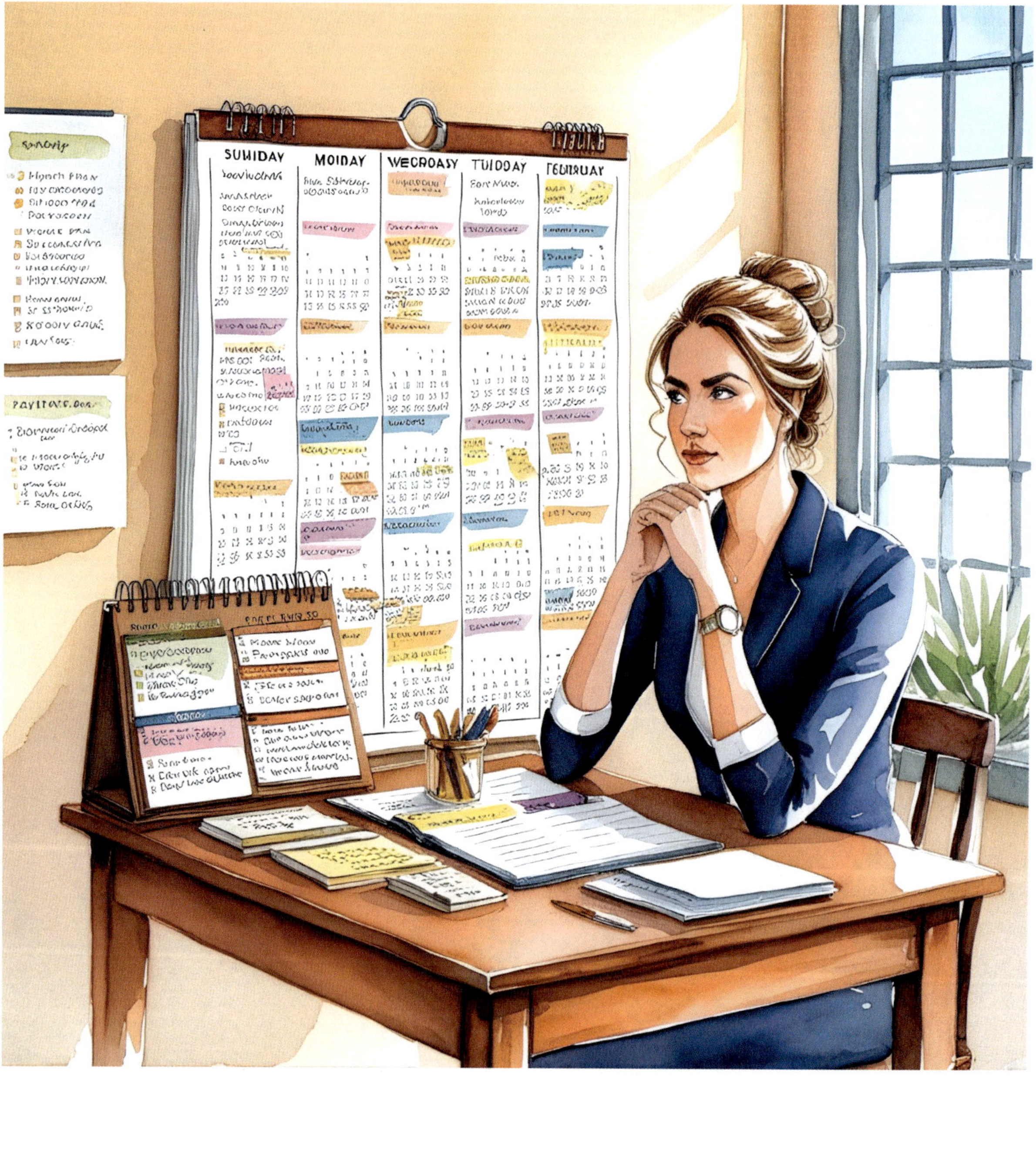

You are
a master
organizer.

You are
a great
communicator.

You are
gentle.

You are
loving.

You are
prayerful.

You are
caring.

You are
brilliant.

You are
an empathetic
soul.

You are
the glue that
holds everything
together.

You are
a jewel.

Made in the USA
Monee, IL
02 May 2025